COPYC

THE ULTIMATE COPYCAT COOKBOOK WITH QUICK AND EASY RECIPES FROM YOUR FAVORITE RESTAURANTS YOU CAN MAKE AT HOME

EMILY CHANG

ISBN 978-1-914144-45-5

TABLE OF CONTENTS

CHAPTER 1: ADVANTAGES OF

HOME-MADE FOODS

All the recipes in this book use key ingredients available in any grocery store—no need to buy fancy equipment because the cooking techniques are simple.

Many key considerations that need to be addressed when building a restaurant experience at home are setting up an enticing table and displaying the food most appealingly. Another advantage of this cookbook is the freedom to adapt the recipes according to your own preferences and diet plans. Foods in restaurants contain more fat, salt, and sugar than our diets need. You may use certain recipes and make your own replacements for a meal free of calories or sugar. Since you already know what the dish will taste like in advance, you know you'll enjoy it before you start cooking. Portion management is a major issue in today's restaurant industry. Every meal on a giant plate is served with the idea that more will be better. Most diet books recommend you eat just half the portion of an entrée while eating out and place the remainder in a box to go. Cooking at home means you can control how many calories you eat. You can also take a break from the meal and a few hours later have cake and coffee, which is something you wouldn't do in a restaurant. Cloning recipes can be an enjoyable activity in which the whole family will take part. In just a sitting, you will be capable of preparing plates from several different restaurants.

With these recipes, the amount of money you'll save will be absolutely shocking. You won't need any special cooking appliances or any special ingredients. If you do any cooking, you probably already have the things you need around your kitchen. Whatever you don't have should be readily available at your local food mart. There's nothing exotic about this. Just a few recipes are all you need.

QUALITY

A team of professional chefs created these recipes. We have checked over and over to make sure you get the exact ingredients and correct steps to make your favorite dish. Of course, you can go online to find recipes that claim to be copycats of popular restaurants. Yes, it's free. And it's a reason they're free. These are not real recipes for copycat purposes. They are actually not even close. I've tried a couple and to be honest, they weren't close, they weren't even good. I'll show you how to get the real copycat recipes and get your freedom back.

FREEDOM

How much time do you waste eating out? Can you get the midnight meal you prefer? When watching your favorite series, will you eat your favorite meal? For instance, you are driving to the restaurant, waiting to sit down, waiting to get your appetizer, waiting to get your meal, waiting to get your dessert and, you guessed it, waiting to pay your bill. How much you did wait? Two hours, three more hours? Take your time and freedom back, and fix your favorite meals at home. Use these copycat recipes when you want to make your favorite meal and how you want it.

IT'S NOURISHING

Nutrition is very fundamental in keeping the brain healthy. This has been proven and emphasized by several mental health organizations. To ensure that your brain remains healthy, nutrition should be a mainstream element of your mental health-care every single day. When you cook for yourself, you become more aware of the things you are ingesting and how those things affect your body. With this knowledge, you will have the ability to control your diet and stay healthy.

IT ENABLES YOU TO HAVE CONTROL

Cooking ensures total control over your dishes. When making your own meals, you have more control over the amount of food you want, the ingredients you want to include in your meals, as well as the amount of salt. When you eat out, however, you give your control away to the chef who will cook the meal. With this control, it is up to you to know and deal with your weight and food allergies as required. In case you are on a special diet because of a medical condition, cooking at home may also be the best option.

IT'S UNIFYING

Cooking at home promotes unity. Yes, when you cook and eat together as a family, you and your family get the time to gather and bond. Members get to share their day's experiences with the rest of the family.

When a family eats together, there is a high likelihood that the children in the family will become healthy, both physically and mentally. This, in turn, causes them to perform better in school, become less obese, as well as reduces the likelihood of substance abuse.

YOU WILL HAVE A COMFORTABLE EATING TIME

When you eat homemade food, you can take the time to savor the meal without wondering if you're wasting time or whether there's a restaurant where your table manners are being observed. Taking time to thoroughly chew your food always makes digestion faster and quicker. I know you may think there's no time each day to concentrate on homemade foods. It might not be easy at the beginning, but there will be encouragement and enthusiasm to try when you consider the things you'll gain. Remember the expression that *"If you don't eat your food like drugs, one day you're going to eat drugs like food."* Don't forget the advantages and health benefits of consuming homemade food if you desire to live long and healthy.

IT SAVES TIME

This idea can sound absurd because many people assume it is always easier to catch a bite at the restaurant when they are on a tight schedule. There are many homemade foods that you can prepare and still enjoy in just 20 minutes (most of the time it takes less than heading to the restaurant).

IT HELPS IN KEEPING A FAMILY TOGETHER

One of the benefits of home cooking and eating is that the family can get together and learn how to share things. Everybody gets the opportunity to share their day during family dinners, their amusing escapades, etc. Often, families who sit down together and eat nutritious food create sensitive and smart kids who don't pursue drug abuse, depression, or have inferiority complexes.

IT WILL IMPROVE YOUR COOKING SKILLS

If you spend little time each day preparing all sorts of food for yourself or your family, your cooking skills will significantly improve. The adage that "work makes good" applies when it comes to cooking. You can start with basic meals and move on to more elaborate delicacies, and you'll cook better than most chefs with time and consistent practice.

COPYCAT RECIPES REALLY HELP YOU LOWER YOUR BUDGET

With a recession scare creeping across the economy and your budget likely getting a very tight squeeze, you're probably looking for some way to stretch it out and make it last. These copycat recipes will help you recover a whole bunch of dollars in your budget!

CHAPTER 2: APPETIZERS

1. CHILI'S CHEDDAR CHEESE BITES

These taste wonderful.

Preparation time: 10 minutes
Cooking time: 10 minutes
Servings: 12

Ingredients:

- 1 pound cubed cheddar cheese or cheese curds
- 1 ¼ cups all-purpose flour, divided
- 1 cup beer
- Oil, as required for deep-fat frying

Directions:

1. Place ¼ cup of the flour in a large resealable plastic bag. Slowly add in the cheese curds and shake until nicely coated.

2. Now, over moderate heat in a deep fryer or an electric skillet, heat the oil. In the meantime, whisk the beer with leftover flour in a large bowl. Slowly dip the cheese curds into the batter and fry until they turn golden brown, for 2 to 3 minutes per side. Place them on paper towels to drain.

2. AUNT ANNIE'S PRETZELS

Aunt Annie's Pretzels has always been a favorite among many people and it is quite easy to make.

Preparation time: 15 minutes
Cooking time: 25 minutes
Servings: 4

Ingredients:

- 2 -4 tablespoons melted butter
- 3 cups all-purpose flour
- 1 cup bread flour
- 2 tablespoons baking soda
- 1 ¼ teaspoons salt
- 2 tablespoons brown sugar
- 1 package active dry yeast (1 ¼ teaspoon)

- 2 cups water
- 1 ½ cups water
- Coarse salt

Directions:

1. Pour lukewarm water in a large-sized mixing bowl and then sprinkle the yeast on top of it; stir several times until completely dissolved.
2. Add sugar and salt; stir several times until dissolved and then add in the flour; knead the dough for a couple of minutes, until smooth and elastic. Leave everything for a minimum period of half an hour and let it rise.
3. While the dough is rising, mix 2 tablespoons of baking soda with 2 cups of warm water; stir often. After half an hour, pinch the dough bits off and roll into a ½" thick long rope and shape.
4. Dip the pretzel into the soda solution; placing it on a baking sheet, lightly greased. Let the pretzels rise for a second time. Bake in the oven until turns golden, for 10 minutes, at 450° F. Brush the baked pretzel with the melted butter. After brushing, sprinkle with the coarse salt.
5. For Aunt Annie's famous Cinnamon Sugar: make a mixture of cinnamon and sugar in a large-sized shallow bowl and melt a butter stick in a separate shallow bowl.

6. First, dip the pretzel in butter, make sure both sides of the pretzel are generously coated with the melted butter, and then dip once again into the cinnamon mixture.

3. OLIVE GARDEN STUFFED MUSHROOMS

If you are a sucker for Italian appetizers, then you have to try this at home: Olive Garden's Stuffed Mushrooms. This meal will make you drool, I guarantee it!

Preparation time: 10 minutes
Cooking time: 25 minutes
Servings: 8

Ingredients:
- ½ teaspoon of minced fresh parsley
- 2 to 3 slices of mozzarella cheese
- 2 tablespoons of minced red bell pepper
- 3 tablespoons of butter, melted

- 12 medium white button mushrooms with their stems removed
- 3 tablespoons of chicken broth
- ½ teaspoon of minced garlic
- 1 tablespoon of shredded Romano cheese
- 1 tablespoon of shredded Parmesan cheese
- ¼ cup of canned minced clams (make sure you drain the liquid)
- ⅓ cup of Progresso breadcrumbs (herb flavor)

Directions:
1. Prepare the oven by preheating it to 450 degrees F.
2. In a medium bowl, mix the Romano cheese, garlic, Parmesan cheese, clams, and breadcrumbs. Mix them well with your hands, then add the chicken broth 1 tablespoon at a time and stir well with a spoon after each addition.
3. Fill each mushroom cap with 1 to 2 teaspoons of stuffing. Make sure to keep the surface flat to support the sliced cheese.
4. Place the mushrooms in a pan (with baking paper on it) with the stuffing side facing up.
5. Brush melted butter over each mushroom, and pour the remaining melted butter into the dish.

6. Add minced red bell pepper on top of the stuffed mushrooms, then place the cheese slices on top. Make sure that the stuffing is covered.

7. Let the mushrooms bake for about 12 to 15 minutes, or until the cheese turns golden brown.

8. When the mushrooms are ready, take them out of the oven and sprinkle ½ teaspoon of minced parsley on top to serve.

4. CHILI'S BONELESS BUFFALO WINGS

These spicy breaded chicken tenders are served by Chili's along with celery sticks and blue cheese, just like the popular wings but without the bone. To make the recipe, you can buy frozen chicken nuggets. Cook as instructed by the pack and then throw in the hot sauce. Use grilled chicken breast for lower-calorie choice.

Preparation time: 10 minutes
Cooking time: 50 minutes
Servings: 8

Ingredients:
- ¼ cup hot sauce
- ½ teaspoon ground pepper

- 2 teaspoons salt
- ¼ teaspoon cayenne pepper
- ¼ teaspoon paprika
- 1 cup flour
- 1 egg
- 2 boneless skinless chicken breasts
- 1 cup milk
- 2-4 cups cooking oil
- 1 tablespoon margarine

Directions:

1. Combine salt, peppers, flour, and paprika in a medium bowl.
2. In another bowl, whisk the egg and milk together.
3. Cut each chicken breast into bite-size portions.
4. Preheat oil in a skillet or deep fryer.
5. Dip the pieces of the chicken into the mixture of the eggs 1 or 2 at a time, then into the mixture of flour/spice. Repeat to double coating per piece of chicken.
6. Once all the pieces of chicken are breaded, place them on a plate and chill for 15 minutes.
7. Drop each chicken piece into hot oil and fry for 5-6 minutes or until golden brown is cooked.

8. Blend the margarine and hot sauce in a small, microwave-safe dish. Microwave for about 20-30 minutes or until the margarine has melted.

9. Upon frying, remove the chicken pieces to a plate lined with paper towels to absorb the excess oil.

10. Place the pieces of chicken inside a sealed dish. Pour the sauce over the chicken, put on the lid, and gently shake until each piece of chicken is covered with sauce.

5. OLIVE GARDEN BRUSCHETTA

The ultimate appetizer in Italian cuisine is without a doubt the bruschetta. It's really not that hard to prepare this ultimate appetizer.

Preparation time: 10 minutes
Cooking time: 55 minutes
Servings: 8

Ingredients:
- Pinch of dried parsley flakes
- 1 tablespoon of grated Parmesan cheese
- 9 to 10 slices of ciabatta bread
- ¼ teaspoon of salt
- 1 teaspoon of balsamic vinegar

- 2 teaspoons of extra virgin olive oil
- 2 teaspoons of diced marinated sun-dried tomatoes
- 2 teaspoons of minced garlic
- 1 tablespoon of minced fresh basil
- 3 firm Roma tomatoes, finely diced (it should be about 1 ½ cups)

Directions:

1. Use a medium bowl to mix the garlic, basil, sun-dried tomatoes, olive oil, vinegar, tomatoes, and salt. Mix well, cover, and then let it chill for about an hour.
2. Prepare the oven by preheating it to 450 degrees F.
3. Use a small bowl to mix dried parsley with Parmesan cheese. Place the bread slices on a tray with a baking sheet on it. Sprinkle the Parmesan cheese mixture on each slice, and bake for about 5 minutes, or until the bread becomes crispy.
4. Take the bread slices out of the oven, put the tomato mixture into a serving dish, and serve alongside the bread slices.

Tip: When you put the tomatoes in a serving dish, be sure to drain the liquid.

6. CHILI'S CHICKEN CRISPERS

This is a great recipe for anyone who loves chicken.

Preparation time: 20 minutes

Cooking time: 15 minutes

Servings: 4

Ingredients:
For Chicken:
- ¾ cup chicken broth
- 10 chicken tenderloins
- ½ cup all-purpose flour
- 1 lightly beaten egg, large
- ¼ cup milk
- 1 cup self-rising flour

- ½ teaspoon black pepper
- 6 to 10 cups vegetable oil or shortening
- 1 ½ teaspoons salt

For Honey Mustard Dressing:

- ¼ teaspoon paprika
- 2 tablespoons Dijon mustard
- ⅔ cup mayonnaise
- ¼ cup honey
- A pinch of cayenne pepper
- 1/8 teaspoon salt

Directions:

1. For Sauce: Combine the entire sauce ingredients together in a small bowl. Using a plastic wrap; cover and refrigerate until ready to use.
2. Now, combine egg together with chicken broth, milk, pepper, and salt in a medium bowl. Whisk for half a minute. Whisk in the self-rising flour and let sit for a couple of minutes.
3. Place the oil or shortening in a Dutch oven and heat it at 350 F.
4. Place the ½ cup of flour in a medium-sized bowl. Coat each piece of chicken into the flour and then dunk into the batter.

5. Work in batches, carefully lower the battered chicken into the hot oil and fry until turns golden brown, for 7 to 9 minutes.
6. Drain on a paper-towel-lined plate or wire rack.

7. FRIED MAC AND CHEESE BALLS

These are very creamy with such intense color! Taste it today!

Preparation time: 10 minutes

Cooking time: 40 minutes

Servings: 4

Ingredients:

Sauce:

- 1 ¾ cups marinara sauce
- 1 ¾ cups alfredo sauce
- ¼ cup heavy whipping cream
- 1 teaspoon garlic powder

- ½ cup ricotta cheese
- 1 cup Italian blend shredded cheese
- ¼ cup red wine

Balls:

- 16 ounces grated white sharp cheddar, grated
- 16 ounces smoked gouda cheese, grated
- 3 tablespoons butter
- 2 tablespoons flour
- 2 cups whole milk, warmed
- 1-pound large elbow macaroni, cooked
- Salt and pepper, to taste
- 3 eggs
- 3 tablespoons milk
- 3 cups panko breadcrumbs
- Fresh Parmesan cheese for garnish only
- Vegetable oil for frying

Directions:

1. Make the balls. In a mixing bowl, combine the shredded cheddar and shredded gouda.
2. In a large saucepan, melt the butter. Add the flour slowly, whisking until there are no lumps. Gradually add the 2 cups of warm milk. Whisk until smooth and continue cooking until the sauce begins to thicken.

3. When the sauce is thickened, remove it from the heat and gradually mix in the cheddar and gouda cheeses. Stir until the cheese is melted and incorporated thoroughly.

4. Add the cooked macaroni and salt and pepper into the cheese sauce and stir well.

5. Butter a large cake pan and spread the mac and cheese mixture evenly into the pan, then place it in the refrigerator for at least two hours. You want the mixture to set and make it easier to form into balls.

6. After two hours, remove the tray from the refrigerator and form the mac and cheese into evenly sized balls about 2 inches in diameter. Cover, and put them in the freezer for at least an hour.

7. In a small bowl, beat your eggs and 3 tablespoons of milk together.

8. Place the breadcrumbs in a shallow dish.

9. In a deep skillet or large saucepan, heat enough vegetable oil so that the balls will be covered when you fry them.

10. When the oil is heated to 350° F, dip each ball in the egg mixture, then the panko crumbs, and drop them into the oil. Work in batches and cook until the balls are a nice golden-brown color, about 3–4 minutes. Transfer to the paper towel as they finish cooking to drain.

11. Make your cheese sauce by combining the marinara and alfredo sauce in a small saucepan. Heat over medium and when warm, add the ricotta, Italian cheese blend, and wine. Stir to combine.
12. When the cheeses have melted, remove the pot from the heat and add the garlic powder and heavy cream. Stir well.
13. Serve the macaroni balls with the cheese sauce and a sprinkle of Parmesan.

8. CHILI'S FAJITA NACHOS

Delicious, crisp nachos get a special twist when topped by a fajita mix. This recipe will certainly be a hit at your next party.

Preparation time: 10 minutes

Cooking time: 23 minutes

Servings: 8

Ingredients:

- 1 Bell pepper, cut into thin strips
- 1 sliced Vidalia onion
- ½ cup shredded Cheddar cheese
- 1 envelope fajita seasoning mix
- 16 large tortilla chips
- ½ cup shredded Monterey jack cheese
- 1 boneless chicken breast, skin then cut into strips

- 2 tablespoons guacamole
- 16 jarred jalapeño pepper slices
- ½ cup thick and chunky salsa
- 2 tablespoons sour cream
- 1 cup shredded lettuce

Directions:

1. Cook the chicken, bell peppers, onions, and in a skillet as per the packet of the fajita seasoning. Drain and set aside.
2. In a large microwave plate, place the tortilla chips.
1. 3.Pace the cooked chicken fajita Layer the cooked chicken fajita on top of the tortilla chips.
3. Add the cheeses over the chicken.
4. Place the slices of jalapeño on the chicken.
5. To melt the cheese, microwave the plate on medium heat for 2-3 minutes.
6. Put guacamole, sour cream, lettuce, and salsa on top of the cheese.

9. AWESOME BLOSSOM PETALS

The ingredients you'll use for this appetizer taste fantastic! It is perfect!

Preparation time: 15 minutes

Cooking time: 15 minutes

Servings: 6

Ingredients:

For Seasoned Breading:

- ¼ teaspoon onion powder
- 2 ½ cups flour
- ½ teaspoon ground black pepper
- 2 teaspoons seasoned salt
- ½ teaspoon paprika

- 1 cup buttermilk
- ¼ teaspoon garlic powder

For Blossom Sauce:
- 1/8 teaspoon cayenne pepper
- 2 tablespoons ketchup
- ½ cup sour cream
- 1 ½ teaspoon prepared horseradish
- ½ teaspoon seasoned salt

Other Ingredients:
- Vegetable oil for frying

Directions:

For Blossom Sauce:
1. Combine the sour cream with ketchup, horseradish, cayenne pepper, and seasoned salt in a small bowl; stir the ingredients well. Cover and let chill in a refrigerator until ready to serve.

For Onion:
1. Peel the onion.
2. Cut the stem of the onion off; place it on the cutting board, stem side down. Cut the onion horizontally and vertically into half, then make two more diagonal cuts.

For Breading:
1. Add buttermilk in a large bowl.

2. Combine flour together with garlic powder, black pepper, paprika, onion powder, and seasoned salt in a separate bowl. Using a large fork, give the ingredients a good stir until well mixed.

3. Put the onions first into the flour and then dip them into the buttermilk; then into the flour again. Let the onions rest on the wire rack.

For Cooking:

1. Preheat oil until it reaches 350° F. Work in batches and add the onions into the hot oil (ensure that you don't overcrowd the onions); cook until turn golden brown, for 2 to 3 minutes.

2. Remove them from the hot oil and then place them on a wire rack to drain.

3. Serve hot and enjoy.

10. CHILI'S CLASSIC NACHOS

Chili's Classic Nachos proves you don't need meat every day!

Preparation time: 25 minutes

Cooking time: 2 hours and 10 minutes

Servings: 5

Ingredients:

- 2 tablespoons guacamole
- 1 boneless chicken breast, uncooked, cut in strips
- A bag of tortilla chips, any of your choice
- 1 cup fresh lettuce, shredded
- ½ cup Monterey Jack cheese, shredded
- 1 package of fajita seasoning mix (1 ounce)
- ½ cup sharp cheddar cheese, shredded

- 1 jalapeño, sliced
- ½ cup your choice salsa
- 1 Vidalia onion, sliced
- 2 tablespoons low-fat sour cream
- 1 bell pepper, sliced

Directions:

1. Over moderate heat in a large skillet; sauté the chicken with onion, fajita seasoning, and peppers. When done, drain the prepared fajita mixture and set aside until ready to use.

2. Now, spread the tortillas out on your ovenproof platter in a large circle. Once done, start layering them with chicken, peppers, and onions. Add the cheeses followed by the jalapenos. Place the platter into the oven and bake until the cheese is completely melted, for 5 to 10 minutes, at 350° F. Once done; pull out the platter and add the shredded lettuce to the center of the chip circle. Top the lettuce with sour cream, salsa, and guacamole. Serve immediately and enjoy.

11. BURGER KING ZESTY SAUCE

Preparation time: 5 minutes

Cooking time: 0 minutes

Servings: 10

Ingredients:

- 1/2 cup mayonnaise
- 2 teaspoons prepared horseradish
- 1 teaspoon cayenne pepper
- 1 teaspoon prepared mustard
- 1 teaspoon white vinegar
- 1 teaspoon lemon juice
- 1/4 teaspoon salt
- 1/4 teaspoon sugar
- 2 teaspoons ketchup

- 1 drop soy sauce

Directions:

1. Combine all ingredients in a bowl and stir until well blended.
2. Cover the bowl and refrigerate for 30 minutes before using.

12. FRIED PICKLES

These pickles are unbelievable, and taste even better!

Preparation time: 5 minutes

Cooking time: 10 minutes

Servings: 4

Ingredients:

- 2 cup pickle chips
- ¼ teaspoon cayenne pepper
- 1 teaspoon sugar
- ½ teaspoon pepper
- 2 cup flour
- Oil, for frying
- 1 teaspoon salt

Directions:

1. Over moderate heat in a deep pan; heat the oil until hot. Now, in a large bowl, combine the flour together with cayenne, sugar, pepper, and salt; continue to whisk until combined well.

2. Drain the pickle chips and then toss them into the prepared flour mixture. Once done, work in batches and fry them (ensure that you don't overcrowd the pan). Once the pickles start to float to the surface, immediately remove them from the hot oil. Place them on paper towels to drain; serve with the horseradish or ranch dressing and enjoy.

13. TEXAS CHILI FRIES

You've never tried something similar! It's insanely good!

Preparation time: 10 minutes

Cooking time: 20 minutes

Servings: 4

Ingredients:

- 1 package of bacon
- 1 bag cheese blend, shredded
- Ranch salad dressing

- 1 bag steak fries, frozen
- 1 jar jalapeno peppers

Directions:

1. Evenly spread the fries over a large-sized cookie sheet and bake as per the directions mentioned on the package.
2. Line strips of bacon on a separate cookie sheet and bake until crispy.
3. When the bacon and fries are done, remove them from the oven.
4. Add a thick layer of jalapenos and cheese; crumble the bacon over the fries.
5. Bake in the oven again until the cheese is completely melted.
6. Serve hot with some Ranch salad dressing on side and enjoy.

14. OLIVE GARDEN BREADSTICKS

Breadsticks are usually served on the side of a dish, but they are also the perfect appetizer or starter. Olive Garden has taken the breadstick recipe and made it perfect. Do you want to find out their secret? Well, take a look below!

Preparation time: 10 minutes
Cooking time: 45 minutes
Servings: 8

Ingredients:

- ¼ cup of softened butter
- 1 ½ teaspoon of salt
- 3 cups of bread flour
- 1 cup + 1 tablespoon of warm water
- ¾ teaspoon of active dry yeast
- 2 tablespoons of granulated sugar

Toppings:

- ½ teaspoon of garlic salt
- 2 tablespoons of melted butter

Directions:

Pour the warm water into a small bowl and add in the sugar and yeast, letting them dissolve. Then let the mixture sit for 5 minutes or until foam forms on top.

In a large bowl, mix the flour with salt, then add the softened butter into the flour using a paddle from an electric mixer. Pour the yeast mixture over the flour mixture, and using a dough hook, blend the ingredients and then knead the dough for around 10 minutes.

Put the dough in a covered container, then let it sit for about 1 to 1 ½ hours until the dough doubles in size.

After the dough has doubled in size, take 2-ounce portions and roll them between your hands to form sticks that are 7-inches long. Place the sticks on a tray covered by parchment paper, cover, and let them sit for 1 to 1 ½ hour until the dough doubles in size again.

Prepare the oven by preheating it to 400 degrees F.

Bake the sticks for around 12 minutes or until they turn golden brown. Once ready, brush each breadstick with melted butter and sprinkle garlic salt on them.

Tip: Set aside plenty of time for this recipe so that the dough can rise as much as required.

15. PEI WEI'S VIETNAMESE CHICKEN SALAD SPRING ROLL

It's time to teach you how to make the best Pei Wei's Vietnamese Chicken Salad Spring Roll! Pay attention!

Preparation time: 10 minutes
Cooking time: 1 minute
Servings: 4-6

Ingredients:
For Salad:
- Rice Wrappers
- Green leaf lettuce like Boston Bibb lettuce
- Napa cabbage, shredded
- Green onions, chopped

- Mint, chopped
- Carrots, cut into 1-inch matchsticks
- Peanuts
- Chicken, diced and cooked, about 6 chicken tenders drizzled with soy sauce, honey, garlic powder, and red pepper flakes

For lime dressing:

- 2 tablespoons lime juice, about 1 lime
- 1½ teaspoons water
- 1 tablespoon sugar
- 1 teaspoon salt
- Dash of pepper
- 3 tablespoons oil

For peanut dipping sauce:

- 2 tablespoons soy sauce
- 1 tablespoon rice wine vinegar
- 2 tablespoons brown sugar
- ¼ cup peanut butter
- 1 teaspoon chipotle Tabasco
- 1 teaspoon honey
- 1 teaspoon sweet chili sauce
- 1 teaspoon lime vinaigrette

Directions:

For Salad:

1. In a large bowl, mix together all of the salad ingredients except for the rice wrappers and lettuce.

For lime dressing:

2. Add everything but the oil to a small container or bowl and shake or stir until the sugar and salt are dissolved. Next, add the oil and shake well.

For peanut dipping sauce:

3. Add all the ingredients to a small bowl and mix to combine thoroughly.

For spring rolls:

4. Place the rice wrappers in warm water for about 1 minute to soften.
5. Transfer the wrappers to a plate and top each with 2 pieces of lettuce.
6. Top the lettuce with the salad mixture and drizzle with the lime dressing. Fold the wrapper by tucking in the ends and then rolling.
7. Serve with lime dressing and peanut dipping sauce.

16. TAKEOUT DRY GARLIC RIBS

These are Indian-style ribs you should make for yourself and your loved ones as soon as possible!

Preparation time: 15 minutes
Cooking time: 2 hours and 15 minutes
Servings: 4-6

Ingredients:

- 6 pounds pork ribs, silver skin removed and cut into individual ribs

- 1½ cups broth
- 1½ cups brown sugar
- ¼ cup soy sauce
- 12 cloves garlic, minced
- ¼ cup yellow mustard
- 1 large onion, finely chopped
- ¼ teaspoon salt
- ½ teaspoon black pepper

Directions:

1. Preheat oven to 200° F.
2. Season ribs with salt and pepper and place on a baking tray. Cover with aluminum foil and bake for 1 hour.
3. In a mixing bowl, stir together the broth, brown sugar, soy sauce, garlic, mustard, and onion. Continue stirring until the sugar is completely dissolved.
4. After an hour, remove the foil from the ribs and turn the heat up to 350° F.
5. Carefully pour the sauce over the ribs. Re-cover with the foil and return to the oven for 1 hour.
6. Remove the foil and bake for 15 more minutes on each side.

17. BOSTON MARKET MAC N' CHEESE

This Boston Market Mac n' Cheese smells unbelievable, and it tastes even better!

Preparation time: 10 minutes
Cooking time: 20 minutes
Servings: 6

Ingredients:

- 1 8-ounce package spiral pasta
- 2 tablespoons butter

- 2 tablespoons all-purpose flour
- 1 ¾ cups whole milk
- 1 ¼ cups diced processed cheese-like *Velveeta*™
- ¼ teaspoon dry mustard
- ½ teaspoon onion powder
- 1 teaspoon salt
- Pepper, to taste

Directions:

1. Cook pasta according to package instructions. Drain, and then set aside.
2. To prepare sauce, make the roux with flour and butter over medium-low heat in a large deep skillet. Add milk and whisk until well blended. Add cheese, mustard, salt, and pepper. Keep stirring until smooth.
3. Once pasta is cooked, transfer to a serving bowl. Pour cheese mixture on top. Toss to combine.
4. Serve warm.

18. CHEDDAR'S SANTA FE SPINACH DIP

You've never tried something similar! It's insanely good!

Preparation time: 5 minutes

Cooking time: 20 minutes

Servings: 6

Ingredients:

- 2 packages chopped spinach, frozen (10 ounces each)
- 1 cup heavy whipping cream
- 2.4 ounces Monterey jack cheese; cut it into 3 equal 2" long blocks
- 1 package cream cheese (8 oz)
- 2.4 ounces pepper jack cheese; cut it into 3 equal 2" long blocks

- ½ cup Sour Cream
- 2.4 ounces White American Cheese; cut it into 3 equal 2" long blocks
- ½ to 1 teaspoon salsa seasoning
- 2 teaspoon Alfredo sauce
- 1 cup mozzarella cheese
- Pepper and salt to taste

Directions:
1. Over low-heat in a large pan; heat the chopped spinach until all the moisture is cooked out, for a couple of minutes, stirring frequently.
2. In the meantime, over moderate heat in a large pot, add in the cream cheese and 1 cup of heavy whipping cream; cook until the cheese is completely melted; ensure that you don't really bring it to a boil. Feel free to decrease the heat if it starts to boil.
3. Once done, work in batches and start adding the Pepper Jack, Monterey Jack, and White American cheeses. Continue to stir the ingredients and don't let it come to a boil.
4. Lastly, add in the Mozzarella cheese and continue to cook.
5. Add 2 teaspoons of the Alfredo sauce and then add in the cooked spinach.

6. Add ½ cup of the sour cream; continue to mix until combined well.
7. Add salsa seasoning, pepper, and salt to taste; stir well
8. Serve immediately with some tortilla chips and enjoy!

19. CHEVY'S MANGO SALSA

It's time to teach you how to make the best Chevy's Mango Salsa! Pay attention!

Preparation time: 20 minutes
Cooking time: 2 minutes
Servings: 2 ⅓ cups

Ingredients:
- 1 mango, peeled, seeded, and diced (roughly 2 cups)
- 2 tablespoons red bell pepper, minced
- ¼ cup white onion, minced
- 1 teaspoon fresh cilantro, minced
- ½ teaspoon habanero pepper, finely minced
- 1 teaspoon lime juice, freshly squeezed

- 1/8 teaspoon salt

Directions:

1. Combine the entire ingredients together in a medium-sized bowl; mix well until evenly combined. Using a plastic wrap, cover and let chill.
2. Serve chilled and enjoy

20. CHEESECAKE FACTORY WARM CRAB & ARTICHOKE DIP

We don't want to spoil the surprise! We'll allow you to discover step by step how to make this amazing dish!

Preparation time: 5 minutes
Cooking time: 5 minutes
Servings: 2

Ingredients:
For Crab Mix:

- 6 ounces artichoke hearts, drained and cut into ¾" pieces
- ¼ teaspoon Old Bay seasoning
- 1 slice of white bread, minced

- ¾ pounds crab meat (backfin or lump)
- 3 ounces cream cheese
- 1 cup heavy cream
- ¼ teaspoon ground black pepper
- 5 ounces sour cream
- ¼ teaspoon cayenne pepper
- 4 ounces mayonnaise
- ½ teaspoon kosher salt

For Bruschetta:
- 4 slices sourdough baguette, sliced ½" thick
- 2 teaspoons breadcrumbs, buttered and toasted
- 6 ounces Crab and Artichoke Mix
- 1 tablespoon olive oil
- ½ teaspoon parsley, chopped

Directions:
For the Crab Mix:
1. Place the cream cheese and minced bread into a large-sized mixing bowl. Pour in the heavy cream and mix until evenly combined. Add the mayonnaise, cayenne pepper, sour cream, old bay seasoning, pepper, and salt into the mixing bowl. Give them a good stir until combined evenly. Add in the crab meat, artichoke hearts, and crab cake mix into the bowl. Gently "fold"

into the other ingredients (ensure that you don't break up any large lump pieces of the crab)

For Bruschetta:

1. Evenly brush both sides of each bread slice with olive oil. Place the bread onto a flat grill (over medium heat) and cook for a couple of minutes, until the slices turn lightly golden and have become crispy. Now, over moderate heat in a sauté pan; heat the crab and artichoke dip until it's warm throughout, stirring frequently to prevent burning.

2. Place the crab and artichoke dip into a small-sized serving bowl. Evenly sprinkle with the toasted buttered breadcrumbs. Slice each piece of grilled bread in half at a slight angle. Place the grilled bread slices and the bowl with crab dip onto a large-sized serving platter. Sprinkle freshly chopped parsley over the bread and crab dip. Serve and enjoy.

21. CHILI'S SALSA

It's an Asian-style dish! It's tasty; it's light and very easy to make at home!

Preparation time: 10 minutes
Cooking time: 10 minutes
Servings: 12

Ingredients:
- 1 can Tomatoes and Green Chilies, Diced (approximately 14.5 oz)

- ¼ teaspoon sugar
- 1 tablespoon canned jalapenos, diced
- ½ teaspoon cumin
- 1 teaspoon garlic, minced
- ¼ cup yellow onion, diced
- 1 can whole tomatoes plus juice (approximately 14.5 oz)
- 1 to 2 tablespoons fresh cilantro, chopped
- 1 tablespoon lime juice, freshly squeezed
- ½ teaspoon sea salt

Directions:

1. Place onions and jalapenos in a food processor; pulse on high settings for a couple of seconds.
2. Add both cans of tomatoes together with lime juice, garlic, cumin, cilantro, sugar, and salt to the food processor; process on high settings again until blended well (ensure that you don't puree it).
3. Using a plastic wrap, cover and let chill in a fridge or refrigerator for an hour before serving. Serve with your favorite tortilla chips and enjoy.

22. JOE'S CRAB SHACK BLUE CRAB DIP

It's such a juicy and delicious dish! You will love it once you try it!

Preparation time: 5 minutes

Cooking time: 25 minutes

Servings: 4

Ingredients:

- 8 ounces softened cream cheese
- 2 teaspoons dry white wine
- 6 ounces lump crabmeat, drained
- 3 tablespoons evaporated milk or heavy whipping cream
- 2 teaspoons chicken soup base or shrimp soup base

- 3 tablespoons parmesan cheese, grated, divided
- 1 ½ tablespoons green or red bell peppers, diced
- 3 green onions, dark green ends, and root ends trimmed, minced
- 2 teaspoons drained salsa or diced tomatoes
- ½ teaspoon Old Bay crab boil seasoning

Directions:
1. Fold the entire ingredients (except 1 tablespoon Parmesan) together.
2. Evenly spread into an oven-proof baking dish and microwave for 4 minutes on half power.
3. Top with the Parmesan and transfer the dish to the oven; broil for a couple of minutes until the top turns out to be browned slightly.

23. SPINACH AND ARTICHOKE DIP FROM APPLEBEE'S

Cooked spinach and artichoke blended with 3 different types of melted cheese... What's not to love about this delicious snack?

Preparation time: 5 minutes

Cooking time: 20 minutes

Servings: 6

Ingredients:

- 1 10-ounce bag spinach, diced
- 2 14-ounce cans artichoke hearts, diced
- 1 cup Parmesan-Romano cheese mix, grated
- 2 cups mozzarella cheese, grated
- 16 ounces garlic alfredo sauce
- 8 ounces cream cheese, softened

Directions:

1. Combine all ingredients in a bowl. Mix well.
2. Transfer into a slow-cooker. Set on high and cook for 30 minutes.
3. Serve while hot.

24. OLIVE GARDEN SPINACH-ARTICHOKE DIP

Are you in the mood for an Olive Garden Spinach-Artichoke Dip? Then you should try this one as soon as possible!

Preparation time: 2 minutes

Cooking time: 35 minutes

Servings: 10

Ingredients:

- 1 can artichoke hearts, drained, coarsely chopped (14 ounces)
- ¼ cup mayonnaise
- 1 package light cream cheese (8 ounces); at room temperature
- ¼ cup parmesan cheese

- ½ cup chopped spinach, frozen
- ¼ cup Romano cheese
- 1 garlic clove, minced finely
- ¼ cup mozzarella cheese, grated
- ½ teaspoon dry basil or 1 tablespoon fresh
- ¼ teaspoon garlic salt
- Pepper and salt to taste

Directions:

1. Combine cream cheese together with mayonnaise Romano cheese, Parmesan, basil, garlic, and garlic salt; mix until combined well.
2. Add in the drained spinach and artichoke hearts; mix until well blended.
3. Spray a pie pan with parmesan and then pour in the dip; top with the Mozzarella cheese.
4. Bake until the top is browned, for 25 minutes, at 350° F.
5. Serve with Italian or French toasted bread, thinly sliced.

25. WHITE SPINACH QUESO

You only need a few ingredients, and you have to follow some simple directions, and you will enjoy some delicious queso in no time!

Preparation time: 5 minutes
Cooking time: 10 minutes
Servings: 12

Ingredients:
- 2 tablespoons flour

- 8 ounces white American cheese
- 2 cups baby spinach leaves, fresh
- ¾ cup whole milk
- 2 tablespoons butter
- ½ teaspoon garlic powder
- 2 cups Jack cheese
- 1 tablespoon canola oil

Optional Ingredients:
- Queso fresco crumbles
- Pico de Gallo salsa
- Guacamole

Directions:
1. Set your oven to broil. Now, over medium-high heat in a large cast-iron skillet; heat the canola oil until hot. Add and cook the spinach until just wilted; immediately remove from the hot pan.
2. Add butter to the hot pan and then add the flour, stir well and cook for a few seconds, then slowly add the milk.
3. Add in the garlic powder; whisk well, then add the cheeses.
4. Continue to stir the mixture until thick and bubbly, for a minute or two, and then, add in the spinach leaves; stir well.

5. Broil until the top turns golden brown for a couple of minutes.

6. Top with salsa, guacamole, and queso; serve immediately and enjoy.

26. TUSCAN CHEESE SPREAD

Your family will enjoy eating this flavored spread! You will love it too!

Preparation time: 10 minutes

Cooking time 5 minutes

Servings: 4–6

Ingredients:

- Tomatoes with balsamic glaze
- 4 Roma tomatoes, finely diced
- ¼ cup red onion, finely diced
- ¼ cup balsamic vinegar

- 1 tablespoon butter
- ¼ teaspoon basil leaves
- ¼ teaspoon garlic powder
- 2 teaspoons Italian seasoning
- Pinch of salt
- Cheese spread
- 1 (8 ounces) package cream cheese
- 1 clove garlic, minced
- ½ teaspoon Italian seasoning
- ¼ teaspoon garlic powder
- ⅓ cup Parmesan cheese, grated
- Ciabatta bread, sliced, to serve

Directions:
Tomatoes with balsamic glaze:

1. Combine the tomatoes and onion in a bowl and cover tightly.
2. In a small saucepan, heat the balsamic vinegar, butter, basil leaves, garlic powder, Italian seasoning, and salt. Heat over medium until the butter melts.
3. Add the diced tomatoes and onion and allow them to heat through. Remove the pot from the heat and cover.

Cheese spread:

1. In a microwavable and oven-safe dish, combine the cream cheese, garlic, Italian seasoning, and garlic powder.
2. Microwave until softened and mix until smooth.
3. Add Parmesan cheese to cover the top.
4. Place the dish under the broiler for 2 minutes, or until the cheese is browned.
5. Arrange the ciabatta slices on the oven rack, and toast.
6. Top the bread with cheese spread and add the balsamic tomato mixture on top.

27. CHILI'S SOUTHWESTERN EGGROLLS

These aren't the typical eggrolls. This recipe contains some typical Southwestern-style ingredients wrapped in tiny tortillas and deep-fried. It can also be made beforehand and frozen for fast, last-minute appetizers if the company drops by unexpectedly.

Preparation time: 10 minutes
Cooking time: 30 minutes
Servings: 8

Ingredients:

- 2 cups washed and drained fresh spinach
- 1 (16-ounce) can drained corn
- 1 (16-ounce) can black beans

- ¼ teaspoon fresh ground black pepper
- 2 chopped jalapeños
- ¼ cup chopped fresh cilantro
- 2 pressed garlic cloves
- ¼ cup minced onion
- ½ teaspoon chili powder
- 2 cups grated Mexican cheese blend
- ½ teaspoon salt
- 15 small whole-wheat tortillas
- Prepared salsa
- Cooking oil

Directions:
1. Combine beans, cilantro, spinach, jalapeños, corn garlic, onion, chili powder, salt, cheese, and pepper in a large mixing bowl, then mix well.
2. Put on each tortilla 2 tablespoons of the mixture and roll into a thin eggroll.
3. Heat a frying pan to medium-high heat.
4. With a tablespoon of cooking oil per 2-3 eggrolls, shallow fry using a sauté pan.
5. Garnish with sour cream and salsa.

28. WORLD FAMOUS CHICKEN CRUNCH

It's such a crunchy and delicious dish! You will love it once you try it!

Preparation time: 10 minutes
Cooking time: 10 minutes
Servings: 4

Ingredients:

- 1-pound chicken tenders
- 1 cup Cap'n Crunch cereal
- 2 teaspoon ground black pepper
- 1 cup milk

- 1 cup flour
- 2 organic eggs, large
- 1 tablespoon granulated onion
- 1 cup corn flakes
- Vegetable oil for frying
- 1 tablespoon granulated garlic

Directions:

1. Pulse the cereals in a blender until you get fine crumbs-like consistency and then pour into a large bowl. Combine flour together with garlic, onion, and pepper in a separate bowl.
2. Beat the eggs and combine them with milk in a separate bowl. Dredge the breast tenders, first into the milk mixture and then into the flour mixture, and lastly into the cereal crumbs.
3. Deep fry until cooked thoroughly, for 3 to 4 minutes, at 325° F. Serve with some Creole mustard on the side and enjoy.

29. COPYCAT MOZZARELLA STICKS FROM TGI FRIDAYS

This is a great recipe for anyone who loves mozzarella sticks.

Preparation time: 5 minutes

Cooking time: 5 minutes

Servings: 6

Ingredients:

- ⅔ cup all-purpose flour
- 2 large eggs
- ¼ cup milk
- 1 cup Japanese breadcrumbs
- ½ cup Parmesan cheese, shredded
- 1 tablespoon dried parsley

- ½ teaspoon garlic salt
- ½ teaspoon seasoning salt
- 8 pieces mozzarella string cheese
- 1-quart vegetable oil
- Marinara sauce

Directions:

1. Add flour to a bowl. Then, in a separate bowl, mix eggs and milk. Add breadcrumbs, Parmesan, parsley, garlic salt, and seasoning salt in a third bowl and mix well.
2. Line baking sheet with wax paper. Set aside.
3. Cut mozzarella pieces in half vertically so that you will end up with 16 mozzarella sticks. Then, for each piece, dredge first in flour, followed by egg wash, and third in breadcrumb mixture. Dredge again in egg wash and breadcrumbs for a thicker coat — Place pieces on a prepared baking sheet and place in the freezer for at least 1 hour or overnight.
4. To prepare mozzarella sticks, preheat deep fryer to 350° F.
5. About 4 sticks at a time, deep fry for about 30 seconds or until golden brown. Using a slotted spoon, transfer to a rack or plate lined with paper towels to drain.
6. Serve warm with marinara sauce.

30. QUESO BLANCO DIP

Are you in the mood for a Mexican dish? Then you should try this one as soon as possible!

Preparation time: 5 minutes

Cooking time 10 minutes

Servings: 10

Ingredients:

- 1 tablespoon vegetable oil
- 2 tablespoons jalapeño pepper, finely minced
- ⅓ cup white onion, finely chopped
- 4 cups white cheddar cheese, shredded
- 2 cups Monterey Jack cheese, shredded
- ½ cup half and half
- ½ cup chopped tomato

- 2 tablespoons cilantro, chopped
- Salt and pepper to taste
- Tortilla chips, for serving

Directions:

1. In a medium skillet, combine the vegetable oil, 1 ½ tablespoon chopped jalapeño pepper, and white onion. Sauté over medium heat until the onion is soft.
2. Add the cheese and half and half.
3. Reduce the heat to low and stir until the cheese melts, then add the fresh tomatoes and cilantro—season to taste with salt and pepper and mix well.
4. Transfer the dip to a heatproof serving bowl, and garnish with the remaining jalapeño.
5. Serve with tortilla chips.

31. RED ROBIN CAMPFIRE SAUCE

Take a look at this recipe, get all the ingredients, and make it for your loved one's tonight!

Preparation time: 10 minutes

Cooking time: 10 minutes

Servings: 6

Ingredients:

- ½ cup mayo
- 1/8 teaspoon cayenne pepper
- ½ teaspoon paprika
- 1/8 teaspoon garlic powder
- ½ cup your favorite BBQ sauce

Directions:

1. Whisk the entire ingredients together until completely smooth; serve immediately and enjoy.

32. RUBY TUESDAY QUESO DIP

A delicious dip that will quickly become a favorite.

Preparation time: 10 minutes

Cooking time: 10 minutes

Servings: 6

Ingredients:

- 1 box chopped spinach, frozen, thawed, and squeeze out any excess water (approximately 10 oz)
- 1 jar of Taco Bell salsa and queso (approximately 14 oz)

Directions:

1. Mix the entire ingredients together in a microwave-safe bowl. Heat in 1-minute intervals on high-power, stirring

frequently. Continue to heat in the microwave until heated through. Serve with your favorite tortilla chips and enjoy.

33. HOUSTON'S CHICAGO STYLE SPINACH DIP

It's a dip that will provide you enough energy to face a busy day at work. Just try it!

Preparation time: 5 minutes
Cooking time: 15 minutes
Servings: 10

Ingredients:

- ⅓ cup sour cream
- 2 bags of fresh Spinach (1 pound each)
- ⅔ cup fresh parmesan cheese, grated
- 1 can Artichoke Hearts, coarsely diced
- 1/8 pound butter
- 2 tablespoons onions, minced
- ½ cup Monterrey Jack Cheese, grated

- 1 teaspoon fresh garlic, minced
- ½ teaspoon Tabasco sauce or to taste
- 1 pint heavy whipping cream
- ¼ cup flour
- 2 teaspoons lemon juice, freshly squeezed
- ½ teaspoon salt

Directions:

1. Steam the spinach; strain and using a cheesecloth; squeeze the water out. Finely chop and set aside until ready to use.
2. Now, over moderate heat in a heavy saucepan, heat the butter until completely melted.
3. Add in the onions and garlic; sauté for 3 to 5 minutes.
4. Make a roux by adding the flour. Give everything a good stir and cook for a minute.
5. Slowly add in the heavy cream, stirring with a whisk to prevent lumping. The mixture would thicken at the boiling point.
6. When done, immediately add in the Tabasco, lemon juice, Parmesan cheese, and salt.
7. Immediately remove the pan from heat and let stand at room temperature for 5 minutes and then stir in the sour cream.

8. Fold in the diced artichoke hearts, Jack cheese, and dry and chopped spinach. Stir well until the cheese is completely melted.
9. Serve immediately and enjoy.

34. LOADED BONELESS WINGS

These Loaded Boneless Wings are not only very tasty!

Preparation time: 30 minutes

Cooking time: 50 minutes

Servings: 10

Ingredients:

For Veggie Queso Dip:

- 1 jalapeno pepper, finely chopped
- ½ yellow bell pepper, finely chopped
- ¼ teaspoon ground cumin
- 1 package American cheese, shredded (6 ounces)
- ½ red bell pepper, finely chopped
- 2 slices of Fontana cheese, shredded
- ½ teaspoon red pepper flakes
- 1 ball mozzarella cheese, shredded (4 ounces)

- ½ teaspoon olive oil
- 1/8 teaspoon each of garlic powder, ground black pepper, onion powder, ground nutmeg, and salt
- ½ cup half-and-half

For Wings:
- 4 strips of bacon or to taste
- 1 package Buffalo-style boneless chicken breast halves, frozen (25.5 ounces)
- ½ pound cheddar cheese, shredded
- 3 green onions, thinly sliced
- ¼ pound Monterey Jack cheese, shredded

Directions:
1. Over medium heat in a large skillet, heat the olive oil until hot. Once done, add the yellow bell pepper together with red bell pepper and jalapeno pepper; stir well and cook for 2 to 3 minutes, until mostly tender, stirring constantly. Add the cumin; cook and stir for a minute more, until the peppers are nicely coated. Add half-and-half; let simmer until almost boiling. Decrease the heat to low and slowly stir in the mozzarella cheese, fontina cheese, American cheese, red pepper flakes, onion powder, garlic powder, nutmeg, black pepper,

and salt. Cook for 3 to 5 more minutes, until the cheeses are melted completely, stirring constantly.

2. Preheat oven to 400° F.

3. Place the frozen chicken breasts on a large-sized baking sheet and the bacon strips on a separate sheet.

4. Place both the pans in the preheated oven. Heat the chicken for 10 to 12 minutes, until thawed; remove from the oven. Continue to bake the bacon for 16 to 18 more minutes, until crispy. Leave the oven on; remove the bacon, place it on a paper towel to dry, and then chop it into pieces.

5. Place a cup of the prepared queso dip into the bottom of a large ovenproof dish or skillet. Arrange the chicken over the top and sprinkle with Monterey Jack cheese and Cheddar cheese.

6. Bake for 5 to 8 more minutes, until the cheeses have completely melted. Sprinkle with the chopped green onion and bacon pieces.

35. FIVE CHEESE DIP

Take a look at this recipe, get all the ingredients, and make it for your loved one's tonight!

Preparation time: 5 minutes

Cooking time: 5 minutes

Servings: 16

Ingredients:

- ½ cup milk
- 1 pkg. softened Philadelphia cream cheese (8 ounces)
- ¾ cup Triple cheddar cheese, finely shredded

- 2 tablespoon parmesan cheese, grated

Directions:
1. Beat the cream cheese using an electric mixer in a small bowl until completely creamy.
2. Slowly beat in the milk until blended well.
3. Add in the leftover ingredients; mix well. Serve with some cut-up fresh vegetables and baked chips; enjoy.

CHAPTER 3: CHICKEN

36. CHICKEN POT PIE

Chicken pot pie is a hearty dish perfect for the wintertime.

Preparation time: 5 minutes

Cooking time: 30 minutes

Servings: 6

Ingredients:

- ½ cup butter
- 1 medium onion, diced
- 1 (14.5-ounce) can chicken broth
- 1 cup half and half milk
- ½ cup all-purpose flour

- 1 carrot, diced
- 1 celery stalk, diced
- 3 medium potatoes, peeled and diced
- 3 cups cooked chicken, diced
- ½ cup frozen peas
- 1 teaspoon chicken seasoning
- ½ teaspoon salt
- ½ teaspoon ground pepper
- 1 single refrigerated pie crust
- 1 egg
- Water

Directions:

1. Preheat the oven to 375° F.
2. In a large skillet, heat the butter over medium heat, add the leeks, and sauté for 3 minutes.
3. Sprinkle flour over the mixture and continue to stir constantly for 3 minutes.
4. Whisking constantly, blend in the chicken broth and milk. Bring the mixture to a boil. Reduce heat to medium-low.
5. Add the carrots, celery, potatoes, salt, pepper, and stir to combine. Cook for 10-15 minutes or until veggies are cooked through but still crisp. Add chicken and peas. Stir to combine.

6. Transfer chicken filling to a deep 9-inch pie dish.

7. Fit the pie crust sheet on top and press the edges around the dish to seal the crust. Trim the excess if needed.

8. In a separate bowl, whisk an egg with 1 tablespoon of water, and brush the mixture over the top of the pie. With a knife, cut a few slits to let steam escape.

9. Bake the pie in the oven on the middle oven rack for 20 to 30 minutes until the crust becomes golden brown.

10. Let the pie rest for about 15 minutes before serving.

37. GREEN CHILI JACK CHICKEN

This dish is hearty and quick to throw together. This recipe is perfect for anyone who is always on the go.

Preparation time: 5 minutes
Cooking time: 30 minutes
Servings: 6

Ingredients:

- 1-pound chicken strips
- 1 teaspoon chili powder
- 4 ounces green chilies
- 2 cups Monterey Jack cheese, shredded
- ¼ cup salsa

Directions:

1. Sprinkle the chicken with the chili powder while heating some oil over medium heat.

2. Cook the chicken strips until they are half cooked, and then place the green chilies on top of the chicken. Lower the heat to low.

3. Cook for 1 to 2 minutes before adding the cheese on top. Keep cooking the chicken and cheese until the cheese melts.

4. Serve the chicken with salsa.

38. CRACKER BARREL CHICKEN POTPIE

This simple, homemade potpie chicken tastes awesome. You will find the perfect comfort food for kids and adults under its golden-brown crust.

Preparation time: 5 minutes
Cooking time: 30 minutes
Servings: 6

Ingredients:

- 2 tablespoons canola oil
- 1 medium onion, chopped
- 1/2 cup all-purpose flour
- 1 teaspoon poultry seasoning

- 3/4 cup 2% milk
- 1 can (14-1/2 ounces) chicken broth
- 3 cups cubed cooked chicken
- 2 cups of frozen mixed vegetables, thawed
- 1 sheet refrigerated pie crust

Directions:

1. Preheat the oven to 450° C. Heat oil in a large saucepan over medium-high heat. Add onion; stir and cook until tender. Season with flour and poultry until blended; whisk slowly in broth and milk. Shift to a 9-inch grained deep-soaked pie plate; place the crust over the filling. Trim and seal the edges. In the crust, put some slits. Bake for 15-20 minutes or until golden brown.

39. DOUBLE CHICKEN PIE

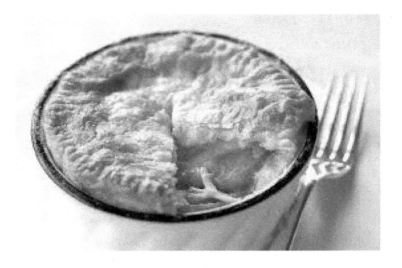

Do you want to discover a classic Southern secret? Well, this recipe is the one you need to check out. The Double Crust Chicken pot pie is enough to dazzle your guests and bring the Southern atmosphere home. The golden crust will win you rave reviews at the dinner table.

Preparation time: 5 minutes
Cooking time: 30 minutes
Servings: 6

Ingredients:
- ½ cup butter
- 1 medium onion, diced
- 1 (14.5-ounce) can chicken broth

- 1 cup half and half milk
- ½ cup all-purpose flour
- 1 carrot, diced
- 1 celery stalk, diced
- 3 medium potatoes, peeled and diced
- 3 cups cooked chicken, diced
- ½ cup frozen peas
- 1 teaspoon chicken seasoning
- ½ teaspoon salt
- ½ teaspoon ground pepper
- 1 single refrigerated pie crust
- 1 egg
- Water

Directions:

1. Preheat the oven to 375° F.
2. In a large skillet, heat the butter over medium heat, add the leeks, and sauté for 3 minutes.
3. Sprinkle flour over the mixture, and continue to stir constantly for 3 minutes.
4. Whisking constantly, blend in the chicken broth and milk. Bring the mixture to a boil. Reduce heat to medium-low.
5. Add the carrots, celery, potatoes, salt, pepper, and stir to combine. Cook for 10-15 minutes or until veggies are

cooked through but still crisp. Add chicken and peas. Stir to combine.

6. Transfer chicken filling to a deep 9-inch pie dish.

7. Fit the pie crust sheet on top and press the edges around the dish to seal the crust. Trim the excess if needed.

8. In a separate bowl, whisk an egg with 1 tablespoon of water, and brush the mixture over the top of the pie. With a knife, cut a few slits to let steam escape.

9. Bake the pie in the oven on the middle oven rack for 20 to 30 minutes until the crust becomes golden brown.

10. Let the pie rest for about 15 minutes before serving.

40. GRILLED CHICKEN TENDERLOIN

This hearty quick-and-easy breakfast wrap makes a perfect start to a great day.

Preparation time: 10 min.

Marinating time 1 hour

Cooking time: 30 min.

Servings: 4–5

Ingredients:

- 4–5 boneless and skinless chicken breasts, cut into strips, or 12 chicken tenderloins, tendons removed

- 1 cup Italian dressing
- 2 teaspoons lime juice
- 4 teaspoons honey

Directions:
1. Combine the dressing, lime juice, and honey in a plastic bag. Seal and shake to combine.
2. Place the chicken in the bag. Seal and shake again, then transfer to the refrigerator for at least 1 hour. The longer it marinates, the more the flavors will infuse into the chicken.
3. When ready to prepare, transfer the chicken and the marinade to a large nonstick skillet.
4. Bring to a boil, then reduce the heat and allow to simmer until the liquid has cooked down to a glaze.

41. BOSTON MARKET'S ROTISSERIE CHICKEN COPYCAT

This simple 5-ingredient roast chicken is done in just five easy-to-follow steps, making a great family dinner during reunions and gatherings.

Preparation time: 5 minutes
Cooking time: 30 minutes
Servings: 6

Ingredients:
- ¼ cup apple cider vinegar
- ½ cup canola oil
- 2 tablespoons brown sugar
- 4 fresh garlic cloves, finely chopped
- 1 whole roasting chicken

Directions:

1. Combine vinegar, oil, sugar, and garlic in a bowl. Add chicken and spoon mixture on top to coat well.

2. Refrigerate overnight, making sure to turn chicken over to soak opposite side

3. Remove chicken from refrigerator. Set aside for at least 20 minutes.

4. Bake at 350° F for about 45-50 minutes or until the temperature reads 165° F on an instant meat thermometer inserted in the thickest part of the thigh without touching any bones.

5. Serve.

42. APPLE CHEDDAR CHICKEN

Your whole family will love it and will ask you to make it more often.

Preparation time: 5 minutes

Cooking time: 30 minutes

Servings: 6

Ingredients:

- 5 cooked skinless chicken breasts, whole or cubed (Cracker Barrel uses the whole breast, but either option works just as well.)

- 2 cans apple pie filling
- 1 cup melted butter
- 1 row Ritz crackers, crushed
- 1 bag extra-sharp cheddar cheese

Directions:

1. Preheat the oven to 350° F.
2. Combine the chicken, apple pie filling, and cheddar cheese in a mixing bowl. Stir to combine.
3. Pour the mixture into a greased casserole dish.
4. Mix Ritz crackers with the melted butter. Spread over the casserole.
5. Bake for 45 minutes or until it starts to bubble.